"How to Achieve Educational Equity
practical call to action that will bene
regardless of where they are in their
created a concrete framework equipt
action towards achieving equity in schools. This book makes inequities - arguably the most insurmountable issue in education to date - feel possible to tackle through courage, collaboration, and accountability. Thank you, Dr. Fields, for your contribution to the field of education!"

— **Dr. Shenita Mayes**, Middle School Principal

"Dr. Fields created a thought-provoking, mindset-changing, eye-opening book on one of the most important topics in today's education. Throughout the book, you can feel his passion for making equity in education a reality for all students. It shines through Dr. Fields' unapologetic challenges to the status quo, traditional approaches to equity in education, complicity, and equity as a "checklist". As an English language learner and a first-generation immigrant, I appreciated the strong, intentional focus on shifting mindsets from the deficit model to the asset model. Dr. Fields provides examples and poses reflective questions that challenges you to be courageous and do what's right for students. Thank you for letting me be one of the first readers of this amazing work!"

— **Dr. Victoria V. Shearing**, High School Principal

"Dr. Fields' natural ability to lead transformative thinking is evident in his latest work. *How to Achieve Educational Equity* challenges outdated equity practices in a way that is profound, yet relatable, and palatable. His work exposes the dangers of oversimplifying such a multi-dimensional concept. This book stretches educators to move beyond the status quo and strive to do more, to be more, and to want more."

— **Dr. Kevin Starks**, Elementary School Principal

"If equity work is going to become more than an idea and make meaningful, assertive progress, then personal reflection, education, and intention must be done by each individual in an organization. *How to Achieve Educational Equity* provides not only tools but teaching for how to do this at each level in a school system. Study this book, reread it, and use it with honesty to not simply talk about equity but make it happen in each facet of your organization."

— **Ms. Jenny Magee**, Elementary School Teacher

How to Achieve Educational Equity

How to Achieve Educational Equity

This book is available at significant quantity discounts when purchased in bulk for educational use. For inquires and details, contact me@drhowardfields.com or 314.643.6393.

Cover and interior design by Howard E. Fields III
Editing by Let's Book Up!

The web addresses and QR codes referenced in this book were live and correct at the time of the book's publication but may be subject to change.

Library of Congress Control Number: 2021906016
Paperback ISBN: 978-1-7369318-1-3
eBook ISBN: 978-1-7369318-2-0
Audiobook: 978-1-7369318-0-6

HOW TO ACHIEVE
EDUCATIONAL EQUITY

Dr. Howard E. Fields III

"Though this is a book about educational equity and
how to achieve it, it is also a book about leadership."

ADDITIONALRESOURCES

AUTHOR'S TALK
Dr. Fields expands on the book and next steps
for how to achieve educational equity.

PROFESSIONAL LEARNING PLAN
A practical framework created for those interested in
continuing to work towards educational equity.

MICRO CREDENTIAL CREDIT
Complete the Professional Learning Plan, along with
a 15 minute presentation and 500 word essay for credit.

MINI PODCAST
Learn from others as they share where they
are on their respective educational equity journey.

EDUCATIONAL EQUITY BLOG POSTS
Access multiple blog posts by Dr. Fields on
the topic of educational equity.

DISCOUNTED CONSULTING
10% off of Dr. Fields' consulting services.

Access these resources at:

drhowardfields.com/EDUequity

To the students, parents, colleagues, and communities who

have ever depended on my leadership, you have always been,

and will always be my motivation.

How to Achieve Educational Equity

Table of Contents

Preface

It means so much, yet so little; depending upon the context in which it is used. You could be in the middle of a meeting or having a casual conversation and hear it suggested as a means to be fair. With the ability to possess the same power as the most heartfelt revolutionary call to action, this six-letter word can also be as meaningless as social justice efforts from a person who publicly protests while simultaneously perpetuating oppressive practices in private. Yet, up until this point; there has not been a consistent rebuttal related to the harm that is caused when this word is not adequately defined or applied with the steadfastness and intentionality necessary to produce desirable outcomes. The word I speak of is *equity*.

Popular narratives continue to wander pervasively with the belief that just by simply mentioning equity, your heart and intentions are automatically aligned and filled with empathy, compassion, and wokeness. Quite the antithesis, from my experiences; such a notion does not capture the duplicitous nature of some who claim to be dedicated to this cause.

Over the last four years, I have extensively studied equity as a construct. It has been embedded within my work as an educational administrator and I have given countless presentations on it at both national and regional conferences. Additionally, I have served on several committees, consulted with multiple organizations, and consistently published work on the topic of equity. More specifically, educational equity.

On February 20, 2021, I co-presented *Eazy E: Oversimplifying Equity and the Harm It Causes* with my brother, Dr. Darryl Diggs Jr. In this presentation, I leveraged years of practical experience, research and quite honestly frustrations to create a definition for educational equity. As evidenced by the feedback on the presentation and requests to expand and continue the work of educational equity, there was a need to take a deeper dive. It seemed that writing a book that would force all of us to grapple with the shortcomings created by not going deeper in our equity work and knowledge emerged as the next logical step in advancing educational equity.

Everything that I have learned as it relates to this often-overused term has been captured and poured into this book. Weekend after weekend, I spent countless hours at the Cambridge Innovation Center (CIC), pushing my mind in a way I have not experienced since completing my dissertation. An attempt to seamlessly convey not only what is educational equity, but how to achieve it, has turned into so much more.

In the pages that follow, you will find things that you agree with, and I am sure; things that you may push back on. What you will not find is fear to speak truth or cowardice that would alter unadulterated truths. Those two qualities alone are all that is needed to allow educational inequities to persist.

Thank you for your time, support, and willingness to continue along your individual journey to achieve educational equity.

-Dr. Howard E. Fields III (🐦@HeFields3)

Foreword

The ability to look across the horizon and admire the vast unyielding skyline, bridging the heavens to the Earth, is a sight to see. As the sun sets in the distance, the sky colors blend into vibrant hues of color, texture, and shapes. The ability to consume the majesty and feel the warmth of the air on their skin is both comforting and complex. Complex in a way, because we experience the world as we know it and continue to build a world that we know it should be. Our current problem requires educational architects to sketch an existence founded on equitable policies, positive student outcomes, and unapologetic results. Like a delicately created sunrise, we know all students do not have the same opportunities to grow to their fullest potential and to feel empowered to be authentic. The most significant detriment to the current education system is that we have allowed this ease to suppress our community's unique perspective and voice far too long.

The imagery I described embodies a person I met in the unlikeliest of places. A needle was found in a haystack with the winning lottery numbers within the wooded depths of a leadership development opportunity. This divine intervention aligned two Black men orienteering, hiking, and canoeing in the middle of nowhere. The probability of this happening in the woods is unheard of and is also common in classrooms across the country. Black male educators are few and far between. The influence of a Black male educator, while invaluable, is frequently absent from our classrooms and all young people's lives. Here, two strangers of different professional backgrounds and personal journeys, found each other secretly battling layers of institutional oppression and self-doubt. Dressed down in all black with black Air Jordan shoes, and a demeanor as cool as the other side of the pillow, it was at this moment I met the embodiment of a real-life unicorn.

Dr. Howard E. Fields III, born to Howard E. Fields II and Lynnette K. Fields, raised in a small area within St. Louis, Missouri called Glasgow Village. Dr. Fields grew up to become a writer, content creator, cinematographer, leader, and unapologetic advocate for kids. Dr. Fields often speaks of the "work" and the meaningful efforts to advance a particular cause that impacts groups of people and their communities. Dr. Fields is a once in a lifetime transformational leader. In 2020, Dr. Fields earned the National Distinguished Elementary Principal Award.

Fast forward to the present day. Amid a leadership orienteering expedition, the man I met cemented himself as a visionary and sought after for his honesty and authentic ability to connect complex topics to actionable processes, concepts, and ideas. In each interaction, I can expect Dr.

Fields to employ extensive attention to detail in the processing of each viewpoint, concept, and action to ensure its benefit for specific communities. Ingrained in each innovative idea comes an empathetic listening ear. Dr. Fields reached out to me when I was at a shallow point in my life. Riddled in fear and professional insecurity, Dr. Fields galvanized the pain I felt and realized this discomfort was unique to other Black male educators across the St. Louis region. In 2019, with Dr. Fields' eyes on the horizon, he and I co-founded Black Males in Education - St. Louis (BMESTL). This endeavor sparked a movement that encompasses groundbreaking symposiums, co-authored books, policy development, mental health seminars, and scholarships. Although we have accomplished a great deal in just two years, our most excellent ideas are yet to come. Dr. Fields is the engine behind the movement, and he unselfishly sees his calling as working towards the betterment of the people.

I am blessed to be able to work alongside Dr. Fields on this journey. We have collectively experienced triumphs, setbacks, and a few detours in the founding of BMESTL and the inception of EduConduits 501(c)3. In each endeavor, detour, pivot, and challenge we faced, I knew something great was approaching from the horizon. I did not think I would find a mentor, confidant, and a friend in the woods, yet I ultimately found a brother.

How to Achieve Educational Equity will challenge conventions and force the uncovering of behaviors that impede our educational system's claim for equity. The first step to any meaningful change is examining the barriers and then removing the connective tissue, which inflames the policies and practices that keep the knee on the neck of our marginalized students and teachers of color. Dr. Fields will articulate actionable steps aimed to uplift necessary change and discard trash equity. Dr. Fields will lead you through a series of steps to uncover, understand, and eliminate inequalities plaguing the education system. Over a century ago, the education system developed skilled workers for industry and factory positions. Now those same learning parameters are employed on 21st-century students who thrive in the digital space. The gaps are widening, the valleys are more profound, and institutional bias and racism is even more prevalent.

The pages of this book will also speak to leaders charged with changing the circumstances of our most valuable assets. If you are looking for practical nuggets to empower your stakeholders, this manuscript by Dr. Fields is dripping with the antidote to cure stagnant growth and educational inequities.

Take notes and enjoy the offering given to us by none other than my brother, Dr. Howard E. Fields III.

- Dr. Darryl Diggs, Jr. (🐦@Achievement4All)

#ACHIEVEEDUEQUITY

As you read **How to Achieve Educational Equity**, connect with others on social media to extend the learning using the hashtag, **#AchieveEduEquity**.

You can also connect with the author, **Dr. Howard E. Fields III** on Twitter at **@HeFields3** or by placing your cell phone camera on the QR code below to access his Linktree.

Dr.Howard Fields.com

HOW TO ACHIEVE
EDUCATIONAL
EQUITY
ActionableEQUITY.com

Introduction

If you Google "Educational Equity," chances are you will see this image. If you ask about educational equity in an interview, most likely this same image will be referenced or described. For so many people, the mental model of educational equity consists of kids watching a baseball game behind a fence while standing on their feet or standing on boxes. The boxes are used as symbolism for resources to help those in need. Such characterization is now the most frequently used illustration to depict educational equity. Though this term is not new, using it within the education context while attempting to make practical strides towards achieving it has become more prevalent over the years. The image, which I will refer to from here on out as the "equity image," has undoubtedly contributed to what appears to be an increase in the number of conversations pertaining to equity. Essentially a reference point, the equity image provides an avenue for reflection, processing, and surface-level dialog about what it means to be equitable in education.

Though it has helped educators and parents grasp the concept of equity vs equality, there are still some apparent and underlying issues when you take an in-depth look at the equity image. Students, especially those who are most reliant on the school system, do not benefit from organizations that embrace the equity image as their vision for equity. Instead, a system built on saviorism that lacks empowerment practices is established. By praising shallow equity efforts and making it more about what is being given to students without seeing what is being taken away from them becomes the culture. This does absolutely nothing for the long-lasting inequities students will continue to encounter as they matriculate through educational institutions.

As a presenter and scholar on the topic of educational equity, I tend to challenge others to go deeper with their understanding and application of equity. In doing so, hearing from attendees as they disclose their frustrations and concerns with how their organization treats equity as a low-level checklist item is a common occurrence. Often, the miseducation of educational equity within their organization, as well as how to achieve it, plays a critical role in stagnant equity practices.

By 2020, my efforts in educational equity included consulting with universities, schools, and nonprofit organizations, working with the Missouri Department of Elementary and Secondary Education (DESE), and implementing practical equity systems and solutions in my role as an adjunct professor, school administrator, and more recently, as assistant superintendent of human resources. Irrespective of the forum, anytime equity is the topic of discussion, follow-up conversations always provide concern for the lack of depth and understanding of "equity" and how to achieve it to impact student outcomes and experiences.

My unique educational experiences allow me to see inequities that others may not have been exposed to or were even conscious of. Through these experiences, I have learned just how vitally important it is to engage in discourse related to educational equity. The more we can watch, listen to, disagree, and process our actions and beliefs regarding equity, the more impact we will have for our students.

What is Educational Equity?

I have used several definitions of equity over the years. Some definitions were from academic institutions and some were from scholars who are considered experts in their respective fields. The more focused my work became, I noticed that equity, specifically within the pre-kindergarten to higher education area, really had not been assigned an adequate definition that spoke to the essence of the term.

Educational equity should be defined as creating and/or eliminating policies, systems, and practices in schools that impact the experiences, outcomes, and access to resources for students from previously excluded groups. Allow me to expound.

Educational equity is more than an image. It is more than being able to watch a baseball game while standing on boxes. Framing it as such, oversimplifies the complexities associated with educational equity.

By taking a closer look at the equity image, you will see that equity is simply being presented as giving to those in need, often described as the less fortunate. While philanthropy is certainly admirable, if one does not reflect on their own personal bias, they could be making some assumptions about the people they want to help. This simply reinforces contributing factors as to why the inequity exists.

In the case of the equity image, the less fortunate title has been assigned to students of color. By providing these students with something they need such as a box, you are in theory; providing an opportunity for kids to see the game who otherwise would not have the ability to watch it.

One of the many problems with this illustration is that it reinforces deficit model thinking. It suggests there is something we must address related to the kids, not the ecosystem they are attempting to function in.

Clearly a barrier, the fence is obstructing the students' vision. Even after a box or two has been provided as a corrective measure, the barrier remains untouched. In one of the more recent iterations of the equity image, the fence has been removed. In my opinion, while this signifies progress; it still does not show equity taking place. The students are still observers, not participants, and they are no closer to the game than they were before the fence was removed.

I vehemently believe the equity image oversimplifies educational equity as a concept. However, I do think the image is accurate when we consider the symbolism and characterization that is depicted.

In education, we tend "not" to eliminate existing barriers within our ecosystem such as policies, systems, structures, and practices that have a documented adverse effect on students. Too often we begin our problem-solving by examining the individual students and not the system that prohibits their progression.

The final aspect of the equity image that I will draw your attention to is the actual game. What if I told you that the students who are shown in the equity image hated they had to watch the game from the outside and stand on boxes, but had to because they were denied admission to the stadium due to their socioeconomic status, ability level, and race? Still wanting to watch the game, they found boxes to stand on and tried their best to move on and not remember how they were excluded and discriminated against. Would your position regarding this image change? Well, here is the curveball, the fact of the matter is that all of us, regardless of our role in the education system, have influence as gatekeepers deciding who enters the stadium. Watching students who are not in the stadium adjust and create their own conditions to experience the game should not be viewed as anything other than a systemic failure on our part, and perseverance and problem-solving on the part of our students.

Regardless, I still see value in the equity image, which is why I would like for you to picture it one more time. We know the image does not adequately convey the definition of educational equity. But what if it accurately depicts something else that is occurring in education. Maybe it is not the students, but the adults who need varying degrees of support to see what is really happening in our schools? Maybe the game being played is not baseball at all but the game of perpetual inequities that many of us can see, but still on the outside just watching while others cannot even see such a game. The equity image, like many vivid images in education, is a snapshot in motion that lacks context to properly understand what is hidden in plain sight. As educators, parents, policymakers, and community members, we must act because currently, the ones with their view obscured is us, not our students.

My Journey

Not hearing my name called during the Riverview Gardens 2002 High School Graduation Ceremony was difficult. I still attended because my cousin was dating one of my former classmates and he wanted me to accompany him. I clearly underestimated the emotional capital I would assert. These were the individuals I attended school alongside since kindergarten. In fact, if one were to look closely at the "02" senior class photo, you would see me. So, you could imagine what I felt the moment I walked pass the line of soon-to-be graduates as they prepared for their big night and heard what felt like half the line acknowledge my presence. I had not seen them in six months.

Four months into my senior year of high school, I transferred to another high school. Though it was not an involuntary move, it was not particularly voluntary either. Being on the varsity basketball team since my freshman year, it was evident that basketball was my identity. Unfortunately, the basketball court was also where I experienced firsthand, the harm adults could cause students.

After being instructed to retrieve a rack of basketballs from an athletic office, I discovered my coach had been opening and throwing away college basketball letters sent to the school with my name on them from interested college basketball programs. Though he would later be removed as coach for a few improprieties, he allegedly had damaging information about the district and threatened to file a lawsuit; as a result, the district reinstated him as coach. For the players who formed a bond with the newly hired basketball coach, the return of the former coach was not good news because many of us would eventually be cut from the team. Caught in between what would later be described as school politics, this leading scorer from the previous basketball season took his talents to South St. Louis County to attend Mehlville Senior High School.

Culture Shock

After my first week at Mehlville, I remember recognizing the concept of educational inequities. Back then, I believe the terms I used when asked to describe my new school was "just different." Comparison through the lens of resource allocation alone and you will notice there could not be more of a difference between the two schools. Riverview was everything that Mehlville was not, and Mehlville was everything that Riverview was not.

Source: Missouri Department of Elementary and Secondary Education. All figures from 2020.	Riverview Gardens High School	Mehlville High School
Per Pupil Expenditure (Local)	$7,671	$8,247
Avg Admin Salary	$79,565	$92,665
Avg Experience in District	7.28 Years	11.86 Years

Going from attending a predominately Black school to only seeing a small portion of Black students was a major adjustment. I must say that even with that, I never felt like I was discriminated against by any of the staff I interacted with at Mehlville. The only race-based incident I remember being involved in occurred in a photography class. As part of an assignment, each student was asked to partner with another student to capture some self-portraits outside. Me and another student, who I will refer to as Nicole, were the only ones who could not find a partner, so we were asked to work together. While outside and clearly not engaging in the assignment, Nicole said to me, "So, I'll take your picture first." I simply smiled and asked her, "how should I pose?" She replied, "Just stand there or act like you're hanging from a noose or something." I did not verbally respond. For the first time that I could recall, my body was having an emotional response that was indescribable. In retrospect, I now believe the surprising and unexpected comment that dazed me for a moment caused a traumatic experience. It was not as hurtful to me as it was perplexing that someone would say that to a person they did not know. Regardless, it was unlike anything I had ever experienced. It was nowhere near the typical "joning" sessions I had countless times with classmates at Riverview. This was "just different."

I also had to adjust to not seeing any adults that were Black. At Riverview, there were principals, teachers, coaches, substitute teachers, and even college recruiters who were Black. At Mehlville, I do not recall seeing any Black adults.

My new basketball coach was a White male, Coach Gegg, and by far, the most caring, nurturing, and trustworthy varsity coach I had played for. In all honesty, my father had given me permission to transfer back to Riverview after the basketball season to graduate with my friends. I declined, in large part because of Coach Gegg.

Nearly 15 years later, I would make another transition to a vastly different educational system.

Time for Administration

In January of 2017, I held a morning meeting to inform my staff that their principal of three years would be resigning at the end of the school year to accept a principal position in a district that was approximately 15 miles away, yet so distant in many respects. Surprisingly, a few staff members cried and would later explain although they were happy for me, there was still a level of sadness and pain. From July of 2014 to June of 2017, Koch Elementary School, the elementary school I attended, located in the Riverview Gardens Schools District, was the most rewarding, accepting, hardworking, and student-centered school I had ever experienced. We were genuinely like a family. In addition to being in an unaccredited school district, among the lowest-performing schools in the state, and with a student transient rate that was the equivalent of an entirely new student body every three years when you consider how many students enrolled and transferred, Koch Elementary was also forced to navigate several crises.

In 2014, the Ferguson Unrest caused by the death of Michael Brown Jr. took place within our school boundary lines and in 2015, the death of Jamyla Bolden, a 4th-grade student who was shot and killed while doing homework in her mother's room on a school night, quickly tested my ability to lead under adverse circumstances. But even in the face of these challenges, our school excelled academically.

In just one year after being appointed as principal, we increased our Annual Performance Report (APR) by 200 percent, the highest growth of any North St. Louis County elementary school in 2015. That same year, we also increased proficiently in English Language Arts by 20 percent and for three consecutive years, our APR increased. We did so well that if individual schools were accredited, we would have been identified as a fully accredited elementary school. What was built at Koch by several individuals still gives me the chills to this day. At the time, our demographic data reflected over 98 percent of the students were Black and 100 percent qualified for free or reduced-priced meals. Approximately 20 percent of students received special education services and our staff was about 55 percent White and 45 percent Black. I provide this data because the common narrative has been, schools like this are not supposed to be successful. Yet, our students showed astounding growth and made it abundantly clear that a dedicated staff willing to have high expectations and intentionality in their instructional practices, along with fearless leadership, is a prerequisite to turn a school around. I will never subscribe to the notion that some students cannot learn because I have seen the contrary.

Though the work of continuous school improvement is never technically complete, my leadership philosophy to build capacity in others also had a lot to do with our success. In my opinion, a school leader who has empowered those around them should create a school where the building can "run itself" in 3-5 years. In theory, at least, by establishing systems and programming that results in higher learning outcomes, yet are run by the students and staff, there is no need for the building principal to micromanage or exert the same amount of energy in management-oriented tasks.

When it was time for me to leave Koch Elementary, I found solace in knowing the school was set up for success upon my departure because of the systems and people that were still there.

Another Culture Shock

When I arrived in the Webster Groves School District as an administrator in the fall of 2017, most of the students were going to be successful regardless of who served as principal. The district's demographics were in large part a contributing factor to this statement. Approximately 80 percent of students were White, roughly 18 percent qualified for free or reduced-priced meals, and about 85 percent of the staff were White.

Source: Missouri Department of Elementary and Secondary Education. All figures from 2020.	Koch Elementary School	Steger Sixth Grade Center
Per Pupil Expenditure (Local)	$5,020	$12,489
Avg Admin Salary	$85,000	$117,209*
Avg Experience in District	7.28 Years	10.55 Years

*Givens Elementary admin salary included in this average. Steger and Givens were in the same building. Steger admin also served as Givens admin.

The immense amount of learning that I experienced was captivated by a recurring theme that would be echoed during my entire three-year tenure in Webster Groves - there are glaring inequities that exist within our schools and school communities. The beliefs and assumptions about previously excluded groups often reinforce negative stereotypes and barriers to enhance learning outcomes for students. This is a quote from a teacher when I began making changes in Webster Groves to enhance learning for all students, "Dr. Fields, you cannot lead over here where most of our students are doing well the same way you led over there where most of the students are not doing well." I found this belief to be pervasive in many affluent spaces. Because many affluent schools do not have to review student outcome data with great regularity, they did not know that many of the students I had in Riverview Gardens were outscoring the students they were consistently failing in Webster Groves. More specifically, the Black students, the students who received special educational services and the students who qualified for free or reduced-priced meals, also known as the student subgroup.

By far, one of the most rewarding experiences I had in Webster Groves while serving as principal at Steger 6th Grade Center and Givens Elementary School (two schools in one building; I was the principal of both) was serving the same family I had at Koch. Two of my students (a brother and sister) moved into Webster Groves and I was fortunate to continue being their principal. This made it easy to not forget where I came from and continue to enact necessary changes for our students who were not being adequately served.

If I had to list the biggest differences between my time as an administrator in Riverview Gardens and Webster Groves with respect to inequities, understand that there are more than a few.

For starters, access to teachers was notable from day one. In Riverview Gardens, an elementary teaching position posting would possibly render 30 or so candidates. In Webster Groves, I frequently saw 300 or more candidates apply for open elementary teaching positions. The impact of this showed up in the years of experience and the advanced degree attainment candidates possessed.

Another apparent difference was financial. The PTO in Webster Groves spent thousands of dollars to help enhance the student experience. But I also witnessed the impact this had on school politics. Because some parents were without a doubt helping the school and district financially, it was not uncommon for these same parents to leverage such influence to perpetuate inequities by impacting the district and school decisions that often did not benefit many of our student subgroups.

The financial variance also showed up in purchasing. Though we had access to some federal monies through Title I in Riverview Gardens that were not available in Webster

Groves, the stipulations associated with Title I funds did not provide as much flexibility in spending. This made, for example, purchasing items such as the responsive spaces and classroom designs in Webster Groves much more difficult to obtain in Riverview Gardens. There was also variance in access to the technology. And when I mention technology, understand I am also referring to the support personnel like instructional technology specialists that play a critical role in ensuring the reliability and effective utilization of the technological infrastructure.

I would be remiss if I did not mention the "elephant in the room," salary. Teachers in Riverview Gardens had been frozen (no additional money or salary raise) consistently for years. In Webster Groves, consistently not providing teachers with raises would not happen. As an administrator there was nearly a $40,000 difference in my starting administrative salary in Riverview Gardens when compared to my starting administrative salary in Webster Groves. With a discrepancy as large as this, it becomes more and more difficult for financially challenged districts to attract and retain effective educators.

One additional difference between these two otherwise "close" districts worth mentioning was the urgency in demonstrating desirable outcomes for students in the subgroup.

Due to my time in Missouri School Improvement Grant (SIG) schools and the Missouri Regional School Improvement Team (RSIT) as being in both a Priority and Focus school (lowest 5 percent of performance), I knew what the expectation was from the highest Missouri education authority. Such pressure to perform in an urgent manner was fine with me. I thrived with this level of accountability. Unfortunately, I have found this is not the norm. Many schools and districts do not adopt this same level of accountability, expectation, and urgency when it comes to showing evidence of growth for students in subgroups. Not only is this concerning, but it also contributes to the need for a more thorough understanding of what educational equity means.

Our Journey

Now that I have provided my perspective along with some of my most vulnerable experiences, I hope you have a better understanding as to why I am so passionate and interested in ensuring educational equity for all students. Like most educators, I value doing what is best for students. But I also value having the integrity to proceed with this practice even when there is immense pushback. It all comes down to leadership. Though this is a book about educational equity and how to achieve it, it is also a book about leadership. We are all leaders, and we all have influence that we must use in a multitude of ways. Many of us are also providers who are responsible for taking care of our loved ones. In the process of being so focused on providing, we typically justify whatever action we need to ensure our families are taken care of. I am asking that you do all you can to see our students with the same promise and care that you view your loved ones. There is no justification for dehumanizing "those kids" or a particular group of people and judging their abilities based on assumptions or limited information you have about them. We are all on our respective journeys. I hope by sharing mine, you will join me in doing all you can to achieve educational equity.

What is Educational Equity?

Educational equity is creating and/or eliminating policies, systems, and practices in schools that impact the experiences, outcomes, and access to resources for students from previously excluded groups. If you are reading equity books, listening to podcasts, or marching with others to protest racism, injustice, or in this case, inequities, you may be on your journey, but these efforts alone do not serve as evidence for achieving educational equity. Neither does hiring a diversity, equity, and inclusion (DEI) specialist. If these types of positions are created with the expectation that the person(s) hired will create and/or eliminate policies, systems, and practices within the organization that impact the experiences, outcomes, and access to resources for those from previously excluded groups, then there is a chance that such a position could help to achieve educational equity. Yet, too often, DEI specialists are set up to fail because they ultimately report to someone who has not done their own

inclusion, diversity, equity, antibias, and antiracism work, or

the organization protects white supremacy by denying any

attempt to address long-lasting systemic issues related to

inequities. We must challenge and pushback on the belief

that the way to address inequities that contribute to

disparities lies in committees, surveys, reports, audits, and

other nonaction-oriented matters that were never meant to

create sustainable change. These time hoarding, emotionally

draining tasks almost always lack the necessary

accountability structure to render any desirable impact. And

for our students whose success is dependent upon robust

shifts in practice, they are left waiting for the next equity

effort while we remain comforted by our good intentions.

There also appears to be a divide in terms of how to

achieve educational equity when you juxtapose the beliefs of

various groups. I once studied this while meeting with two

different groups of leaders. One group consisted of high-ranking district and state officials and the other was comprised of leaders who were Black educators. When asked what was needed to further equity work, a DEI position was the most frequently recorded response for high-ranking officials while the Black educators pleaded for accountability and other quantifiable outcomes. This is more of a reason why we must define educational equity and be clear on what we are attempting to accomplish.

Educational equity is action - unapologetically creating and/or eliminating policies, systems, and practices. Think about what former Dallas Cowboys fullback, Daryl Johnston used to do on the football field. His role on the team included blocking those who were serving as barriers to Hall of Fame running back, Emmitt Smith's progress. Daryl flourished in this role. This is the image we should be using to illustrate what we need to do for previously excluded students within our schools. Until we reframe our thinking and begin viewing educational equity as action, we will continue to miss the mark We must ask ourselves a lot of reflective questions. As a collective, are we blocking and removing those discipline policies that disproportionately impact our students in the subgroup? Are we removing barriers for previously excluded groups of students so they can proceed into advanced and gifted courses? What about those one-sided, single-story, Eurocentric curricula that do not promote the organization's goal to prepare students for a global and diverse society? Are we creating pathways to reinforce the importance of diversity by embedding it in the lessons, curriculum, materials, books, and authors? We have been neglectful in our teachings, which perpetuates inequities and sometimes, racist ideology. For example, by only showing Black people in subservient historical contexts or when it is Black History Month, the educational system communicates a particular narrative about what it means to be Black and where we come from. Rather than showing your support in a social media post, it would be more impactful if you helped to implement a Black History Month program or teach students about what life was like for Black people prior to the Transatlantic Enslavement. Though equity is not only confined to race, to ignore it simply strengthens the point that we have been excluded from so many tables where educational decisions have been made. Another reflective question we should ask ourselves has to do with hiring processes. Are we challenging and removing those comments about "fit" or the practice of only hiring people of color when there is a consensus? Historically, this has meant the person of color who "fits" is not threatening and shares many of the values and beliefs already upheld within the organization. If you are not creating or eliminating, your equity efforts are considered trash equity- superficial or surface level efforts that are built on deficit models. These non-quantifiable, non-systemic practices typically lack accountability and thus do not impact the overall experiences, outcomes, and access to resources for students from previously excluded groups.

I am sure by now you have noticed the usage of the phrase, "students from previously excluded groups," as opposed to "underrepresented students." This is intentional. I do not believe the term "underrepresented" adequately conveys what has historically occurred in our country and in our schools when it comes to educational inequities. To be underrepresented could be interpreted as a lack of interest. This allows the falsity and proverbial response when asked about the lack of diversity in hiring, advanced classes, books, etc.-, "we tried but couldn't find any people or students of color" - thus they are underrepresented. Previously excluded is a more precise phrase. We have been excluded because of actions and inactions by a system. Such action and inaction have consciously and subconsciously occurred. Regardless, the lack of interest, skill, and anything else other than a lack of opportunity is a defense mechanism established to allow good intentions to suffice. Previously excluded is also included as a foundational block to educational equity because I think it is critically important to understand, you cannot be equitable if you are excluding people. It is impossible.

The Barriers

Given the way educational equity has been defined in this book, I understand that prior to achieving it, we must have a solid understanding of barriers that are associated with educational equity. Our biggest barrier in this work has been ourselves. Every time I have presented equity content, I posed this question, "How have you been complicit in the perpetuation of inequities?" The same themes seem to always

emerge. Respondents typically report that they were too

afraid to challenge supervisors, concerned about potential

pushback or retaliation for speaking up, or have fallen into a

perpetual state of accepting things as the way they are, even

if they know and admit students are being harmed because of

their inaction. When I follow up and ask them to identify

additional barriers standing in the way to achieving

educational equity, once again, respondents typically were on

the same page, citing their superintendent, Board of

Education, fear, politics, defensiveness, lack of awareness,

complacency, and not knowing how to start.

In the next chapter, I will begin unpacking a formal

process for achieving educational equity. But before I do, I

want to frame my efforts in the most deliberate and

attentional manner. My recommended approach to

educational equity, optic-wise, is in alignment with the safety protocols we are encouraged to use while navigating the COVID-19 global pandemic. Like the pandemic, educational equity is complex and requires the same level of intentionality and care.

Initial Action Steps

The 6 initial action steps for achieving educational equity are as follows:

- *Step 1: Ask Yourself, "Am I Being Complicit in Educational Inequities?*
- *Step 2: Identify Educational Inequities*
- *Step 3: Challenge Existing Equity Efforts & Barriers to Strengthen/Systematize*
- *Step 4: Throw Away Superficial, Trash Equity*
- *Step 5: Wash Your Hands*
- *Step 6: Repeat Steps 1-5 and Bring a Friend*

Step 1: Ask Yourself, "Am I Being Complicit in Educational Inequities?

If you are being honest with yourself, the better question is, "How am I being complicit in educational inequities?" This self-reflective question must always be at the forefront of our minds as educators. Educational inequities can insidiously permeate our systems when we are not reflective. Unfortunately, I have been disappointed so many times in well-intentioned colleagues and parents who truly believe they are creating equity in our schools, yet they do not see or fail to acknowledge how their actions or inactions harbor inequities.

I once had a colleague ask me what they could do to assist with addressing educational inequities. After a brief pause, I informed this person that it was important to use their voice and speak out when students are being harmed by policies, systems, practices, and sometimes adult behavior. This person stated that they wanted to act but did not want to fracture the strong relationships they had with colleagues. When I asked why they were choosing adult relationships over student success, this person presumed my question was a rhetorical one when I was actually interested in hearing their response. The conversation ended shortly after.

Though it may be easy for you to judge my former colleague, the purpose of providing you with this illustration is to reiterate how important it is for us to have a sense of self-awareness as a means to determine how we are being complicit in educational inequities. For schools and districts with a relatively low percentage of subgroup students, if they are already considered high performing, they may not feel the need to change their practices, even if these same particular groups of students are not performing as well.

When I transitioned as an administrator from Koch Elementary to become an administrator at Steger and Givens, though I was an instructional leader who was accustomed to enhancing learning outcomes for students, I found myself in a constant battle with well-intentioned instructional minded educators who were comfortable in their roles and did not think it was necessary to change systems that were not good for all students. Few were able to see how this contributed to complicity.

Another way that educators are complicit in educational inequities is undermining the process because they want the credit or have a personal issue with the person(s) leading the equity work. In addition, some equity efforts have failed due to the timing of its implementation occurring during a political season. I have also witnessed equity efforts fail due to a scarcity belief. For some, achieving educational equity means taking away from others and this could not be further from the truth.

The most concerning, however, has been witnessing adults who were previously excluded as students either choose silence or attempt to justify inequities out of fear of being viewed as ungrateful by an oppressive system. (Read that last sentence again.)

What makes this first step along with the following five steps so difficult, is that most educational organizations do not embrace a culture of challenging the way things are done nor do they request the necessary evidence to substantiate the effectiveness of their existing practices.

Before you proceed, please know that simply not having the difficult conversations or failing to ask the tough questions will not lead to educational equity. At the same time, if you have created a punitive culture based on fear where people are afraid of being reprimanded for pushing back or asking for clarity, you may be the reason educational inequities exist within your organization. The best way to check is to ask yourself, "How am I being complicit in educational inequities?" An honest response will help you and ultimately our students if you proceed accordingly.

Step 2: Identify Educational Inequities

Do not ask yourself if educational inequities exist in your organization because they do. In this step, you must take the necessary time to identify the policies, systems, and practices in schools that impact the experiences, outcomes, and access to resources for students from previously excluded groups. Please know that this is not an easy task. If you are benefitting from the system or have not had any major issues, you may not be able to identify inequities. It is precisely because of this that I recommend conducting listening sessions. Organize at least three separate groups: a group of students who have been previously excluded, a group of parents whose children have been previously excluded (try to select parents you normally do not hear from), and a group of teachers or educators who have been previously excluded. Even if you cannot form such groups due to the makeup of your school community, work to make it happen virtually with people who do not reside in your community. Once the groups have been created, simply ask them to identify educational inequities within your school or community. Your only role after asking this question is to listen. Listening sessions are quite impactful as a form of staff development.

Now that you are aware of some inequities that exist within your school community, ask yourself, "Why do these inequities exist?" Be prepared to ask more why questions and drill down through the surface to obtain a better understanding. As educators, we are problem solvers. What this means is that many will want to begin working towards solutions right away, but I think it is important to take some time to adequately reflect and process the identified inequities and why they exist. Try to spend some time understanding who is benefitting from these same inequities and why. This is a critically important aspect of achieving educational equity because it will help you better understand and respond to the pushback you will without a doubt receive when you decide to proceed.

I ask that you spend a significant amount of time understanding deficit models and asset models as it pertains to students and what they need. The reason why the equity image was so widely used and well-received is because it is a mental model that so many of us have with regards to how we see and respond to inequities. Economist James Andreoni once stated, "If giving feels good, how generous can it really be? Maybe gifts are just another way of using other people to make ourselves feel good." Giving to a "needy" child is the most exhilarating feeling for some. There are countless educators and organizations that are celebrated for the amount they give. But what happens when the identification of who is needy as well as what is given is steeped in deficit model thinking and perpetuates inequities? By viewing those kids as only needing a hug, or food, or a loving environment, you may be insinuating that they do not already have those things. In addition, while you are increasing your empathy for the students, you may also be increasing your disdain for the parents and communities they come from. Although some students need basic necessities in order to succeed, I have never met a student that had more needs than strengths and positive attributes. When identifying inequities within your school, know that those same students who are being held back by inequities have strengths that you can build upon as a means of helping them thrive. It just often requires you to remove the deficit lens you have been socialized to look through.

Step 3: Challenge Existing Equity Efforts & Barriers to Strengthen/Systematize

In 2021, the overwhelming majority of educational institutions are doing something in the name of equity. But is it addressing the identified inequity at its core? Take those same inequities that you identified in Step 2. Now review all the equity initiatives, policies, efforts, books studies, statements, etc., that exist within your organization then attempt to answer the same question, "Are the existing equity efforts within the organization getting to the core of the identified inequity?" No need for an extensive amount of think time because the answer is most likely no; especially when we have not drilled down to determine what is the root cause of the inequity.

Based on my experience, most equity efforts are nonexistent, hidden within documents on the website and main office, or surface/superficial. All of which is extremely harmful to students. If I could create a bumper sticker aligned to this step, it would read, "Nonexistent and Surface Equity is More Harmful Than Accidents." When this occurs, equity becomes a checklist item, and seldom does it ever evolve into meaningful practices.

As part of this step, try to determine why the existing equity efforts are not more effective in addressing the identified inequity. Are the issues due to a skill deficit or will deficit? Do the individuals within the organization lack the skill required to achieve educational equity or do they lack a willingness to address the inequities? If it is a skill deficit, professional learning opportunities along with this book will be helpful. If it is a will deficit, you have a bigger problem that will test your leadership and the leadership within the organization.

Step 4: Throw Away Superficial, Trash Equity

If your equity efforts/solutions are not quantifiable, focused on systemic shifts, adequately funded and supported, and focused on removing barriers associated with previously identified inequities, throw it away, it's trash!

I use such aggressive and polarizing language because, in education, we tend to hang on to outdated and ineffective practices way too long. This can be the result of many contributing factors but it all boils down to our field being slow to change unless it is forced. In the spirit of this, we must force others to see the harm in continuing these archaic practices. Though I love to read and discuss with others, book studies alone as a strategy to address inequities is trash. If some type of intentional action such as creating or eliminating policies, procedures, or systems does not occur during the book study or shortly after, again, it is trash.

Another superficial, trash equity practice is creating a new committee or meeting just to receive an update on how the organization is still not serving all kids. Imagine promising your school community that you are going to build a community center for students to help them be more active. Once you started to get to work, you noticed how much more difficult the task was. So as a strategy, you schedule meetings with the community to let them know how much more difficult of a task this is. A few months later, you schedule more meetings to talk about why it is so hard. Then you review not only why it is so hard to build a community center in your community, but you provide data on why community centers are just too difficult to build.

When this becomes the practice of the organization, you are no longer meeting to problem-solve a way to proceed, you are meeting to provide an updated excuse as to why progress is not being met. Though I am being slightly facetious, what I just described has been listed and accepted as a viable strategy for not addressing inequities in our schools. Due to no one challenging or pushing back in instances like this, I do not know if the organization realizes that this practice is trash. Chances are they know it is not enough to achieve educational equity, but they sell the perception of progress anyway because it is safe and comfortable. Regardless, it is trash. Recyclable, maybe, but still trash.

Step 5: Wash Your Hands

"Wash" your hands is actually W.A.S.H. your hands. W.A.S.H. is an acronym for a protocol used to work towards educational equity. Arguably the most important step, this is where the most change occurs.

W.A.S.H. stands for *Work, Anticipate, Strengthen,* and *Help.* Once you acknowledge how you have been complicit in educational inequities, identify the educational inequities that exist within your organization. After this, challenge and throw away ineffective equity efforts. It is now time to get to work.

Work

Given what you know, how are you planning to create and/or eliminate policies, systems, and practices that impact the experiences, outcomes, and access to resources for students from previously excluded groups? Regardless of your role or title, you certainly have influence that you can leverage to get to work. It is important to understand that when you are at Step 5, as long as you get to work by doing something that is action-oriented and aligned with the educational equity definition I have provided, you cannot go wrong. While doing the work, take a lot of notes and reflect on everything. Over articulate what you are attempting to do and why. As you will learn throughout Step 5, those who provide pushback will take your words and actions to create confusion and barriers to achieving educational equity. Remember, many people benefit from inequitable systems so changing such systems will be viewed as a threat to their dominance.

Anticipate

I just recommended that you write things down, over articulate what you are trying, and why you are trying to do it because pushback is coming. I have learned that instead of getting mad and frustrated when this occurs, anticipating it can strengthen the likelihood that you will be able to enact change that can have a positive impact on our students.

Educational systems are predictable. In business matters, it is often said that watching the money will tell you all you need to know. When it comes to being engaged in equity work, all you need to do is listen to what people consistently say, then watch what they consistently do. Everything you need to know about that person such as what they value, how they operate, and what are their fears and motivations can be gleaned from observing and listening.

As a fundamental belief, equity is widely accepted. But once action is enacted to achieve such equity, pushback will occur. Those who pushback will attempt to take your words and actions to create confusion. Rest assured this is very intentional and quite effective. I have been able to overcome this strategy by referring to documents, statements, dates, and data that reinforce what I am attempting to do and why.

Strengthen

Once you have received pushback, take a bow; you will know and feel the exhaustion that comes with being engaged in equity work. It is at this time that you will have to strengthen your plan. Hopefully, the pushback, and sometimes criticism, was recorded. You will need to review and reflect on it. Get used to being scholarly in your approach. Do your homework. Find research to challenge misconceptions and assumptions. Determine the logistics and support needed to ease anxiety. Call out things that have been shared to halt or prohibit progress. But most importantly, show that you took all feedback, concerns, and suggestions to strengthen your case while also breaking down nonsensical matters that are illegitimate.

Help

If you are not tired yet, you will be. Remember to help yourself. Leading or being engaged in equity work is some of the most exhausting work you will do in education. Make sure you have a support group and a way to adequately process and reflect. There are a number of equity warriors who eventually succumbed to the associated demands because they were not able to help themselves once the turbulence caused by disrupting systems became too much to bear. Discover a passion that can be used as an outlet. Sometimes you will simply just need to unplug. But most importantly, make sure to help yourself by being true to who you are and providing yourself with grace. This will be a long and bumpy road at times.

Step 6: Repeat Steps 1-5 and Bring a Friend

Once you have successfully created or eliminated a policy, system, or practice that impacts the experiences, outcomes, or access to resources for students from previously excluded groups, you should find a way to celebrate. Having experienced this feat several times, I can attest to this being a different level of fulfillment. Understand that your work is not done yet. Given the number of inequities that remain in education, we need to do all we can to help as many people as possible get involved and use their influence to achieve educational equity.

Though this section prompts you to bring a friend, know that through my experience leading equity work, I was able to convert a few former critics into supporters. Such a testimony from someone who was at one point critical of equity work can impact individuals that would never be open to listening to me. In the words of Amy Hunter, sometimes we should not call people out, but call them into the work. I actually believe there is a time to do both, but I certainly understand the premise and believe it applies here.

Application of the Initial Action Steps

Now that you are familiar with each of the 6 steps, I will provide you with a practical example of how I applied each step at the teacher level, principal level, district level, and state level. You will notice the progression of my equity efforts over the years, which should serve as a reminder that we all have influence that we can use to advance educational equity.

Teacher Level

As a teacher, I was complicit in inequities by subscribing to the "us" and "them" type of thinking - us teachers vs them students. This was evident in the way we attempted to hold students accountable. One such practice included leveraging physical education class for work completion. If students did not finish their homework or class work, they were held back from physical education class. If it was towards the end of the year and there was an abundance of missing work, the student may have missed their field day. Now, you may be thinking, "I've used this practice as well. What makes it a matter of educational equity?" Regardless of the intent of the practice, the same students were the ones missing physical education class and field day. These students were also the ones with the most challenging home dynamic. It was this realization that created awareness that educational inequities, do not require malicious intent.

When I started to question this practice, which had been in place for years if not decades, a lot was discovered. This was not a policy or even a procedure that was approved by administration. This was simply a practice that was communicated with parents at the beginning of the school year as an expectation. Because we had previously made annual yearly progress (AYP) and this practice was touted as a reason why students were achieving academically, it was accepted. The guilt I continued to bear watching so many students that looked like me cry out for help through the stare and glare of their eyes is what forced this new teacher to W.A.S.H. his hands.

A few months into my first year of teaching, I banned the practice of students missing physical education class to complete assignments. The tipping point came when a parent asked me about a first quarter grade for a student that I had not seen all quarter. I would later find out that the student was enrolled, he just had not come to my class for the entire quarter. Though there was pushback from a few grade levels, most staff understood and even recognized that this practice was probably outdated. I strengthened this decision by making staff aware that if students missed physical education class, I would need to pull them from a core content area to make up for the missed time and ensure their physical education grade was accurate (some staff did not realize students earned actual grades in physical education class).

This newer practice appeared to be a win-win, but I knew I could do more. In collaboration with the teachers who were struggling the most with this change, I worked with them to help reinforce the importance of work completion while also leveraging the class they loved (the instructor they loved as well).

After several conversations, I was also successful in helping some of my colleagues understand that we were punishing kids for their home dynamics. An assumption was being made by "us" that students were being disobedient when they did not complete assignments. We were ignoring the complexes in learning, motivation for learning, and the ability to complete work when they exited our school. These efforts would prove to be time well spent because eventually, students missing any class to make up work for another class became an anomaly. If you were wondering, yes, some of my colleagues who were now supportive of this change still struggled when I refused to allow them to use field day as a punitive measure for minor behavior incidents. The next step was forming a coalition to stop using recess as a behavior management strategy. As you can imagine, this would be much more of challenging task.

Principal Level

As a principal, I was complicit in inequities by thinking because I was new, I should not start enacting change right away. This was my mindset until I identified an inequity that forced me to act. I resolved that not acting felt like educational neglect. So ultimately, I decided to challenge the identification process for gifted education after it was discovered that many of my Black students were consistently not being identified as gifted.

Whenever there is a lack of representation, it has been my experience that bias in the selection process or non-commensurate dynamics such as access to information or social networking capital plays a major role. In this case, all of these were in play. The current practice heavily relied on teachers or parents to recommend gifted testing. Though this was well intentioned, it created an inequity that rewarded students whose teacher viewed them as gifted or students whose parent/guardian had the information. There is no shortage of research that Black and Brown students are not viewed as intellectuals at the same rate as their White classmates. Combine this with the fact that some parents, by virtue of their home dynamics or proximity to the school, are informed and reminded of school related matters more often than others. These parents are also more likely to be encouraged to nominate their child(ren) for gifted testing.

The decision to challenge this system was difficult.

Challenging any system in the name of equity can be

difficult. Complicity continued to seep in my mind. Not only

was I new and used that as my rationale not to do anything,

but I also did not want to change everything so soon because

we were way ahead of other school systems with regard to

our equity efforts; at least on the surface we were.

By the look at our Equity statements, social media,

and intent to serve all, we were equity champions. But in

practice, across the system, we were as inequitable as other

school systems. I ultimately decided to W.A.S.H. my hands.

It was quickly determined that students' teachers

from the previous school year played a larger role than I

originally thought in the identification of giftedness. The

term quality of work was reintroduced to me in my

investigative efforts of the criterion used for recommending

students for gifted testing. In my mind, in a district as well-resourced as the district I was in at the time, I wondered why we could not simply test all of our Black students for giftedness. When I proposed this plan, there was some pushback. Rather than shut down and toss the idea, I carefully listened to the concerns to strengthen the next proposal related to this matter. A structural barrier to recommending a bulk of students for gifted testing all at once was the submission form. Each form required the student's name, address, teacher, a brief rationale for the testing request, and a signature from the person making the recommendation. Even with what felt like a deterrent, I had a great idea. As a data spreadsheet savant, I knew there was a way around this, but I had to decide if it was worth upsetting a few of my colleagues due to the added work of testing more students than they may have been accustomed to and engaging in what could be perceived as showing them up. I want to pause at this moment because all educators have experienced or will experience this exact dilemma. We all understand the importance of relationships in our work. But please rest assured that a relentless focus on putting students first will in fact result in fractured relationships with adults. However, sometimes this is the price you pay for student-centered and equity-focused leadership. I would rather have an adult upset at me for doing the right thing for kids than the reverse any day of the week. Let us concede the fact that all educators love their students and want them to succeed. The more relevant question is, are they willing to challenge, and ultimately correct the actions or inactions of other adults to ensure such success for students will occur?

While going through this, I helped myself by having a support group of thought partners that I could count on to remind me that student-centered and equity-focused is student-centered and equity-focused, regardless of the location or person(s) in the room. This is of priceless value when you may be questioning your leadership.

Reflecting on this matter years later, it is still one of the highlights of my time as a principal. All Black and Brown students who entered our school having scored in the proficient or advanced category on their previous MAP test (any subject) were recommended for gifted testing. Many of which would be accepted into the gifted program. While a few staff members were not fans of mine as a result, some previously silent staff members would help spearhead subsequent building-wide equity work.

District Level

As a first-year district administrator, I remain complicit in inequities. Even with all the experience I have along with being a published author on this topic, I constantly have to challenge myself to continue working towards achieving educational equity. Being a Black male in education, the narrative is that I am a disciplinarian and passionate when discussing equity. The unintended consequence, however, is we are not often viewed as nurturers or instructional leaders. Unfortunately, this has created a dynamic that forces me to consistently remind myself of what I know to be true-- I am all of the above; more than just someone who seeks to reach educational equity. I have made a concerted effort to not be viewed as the one who brings attention to all the inequities. Conversely, my vantage point allows for observing inequities in education as often as I hear the pledge of allegiance. I believe that having a seat at many tables comes with a level of responsibility to advocate. If I were to be silent on such significant matters, it would be the highest level of betrayal to the students, staff, and communities that I have served.

A benefit to working in Human Resources while also working towards educational equity is that you are put in a prime position to impact systems. I am currently leading efforts to examine what equity within the interview process entails. By doing so, we are pushing back on the role of "fit" and consensus in hiring. Though equity has been a focal point for some time, a deliberate and sustainable plan with embedded accountability measures continues to be a work in progress.

As it relates to hiring, diversity fairs are often pointed to as an existing practice to enhance equity (through representation). Feedback from years of diversity fairs have revealed concerns in what they have become. Many participants feel as if the hiring of people of color started to feel transactional and encouraged assimilation as a means of employment. Additionally, without a large influx of candidates of color entering the education field, it was often found that those who were hired were either leaving schools

that served a high percentage of Black and Brown students,

or they were leaving another school system searching for

diversity but could not adequately support the diversity they

already had. The most effective recruitment strategy is

retention. And so, in an attempt to take existing feedback and

apply it in a meaningful way, I made the decision to do away

with the more traditional diversity fairs in exchange for a

networking event where we focused on empowering potential

job seekers as well as our current staff of color. Making

provisions with professional learning as it pertains to

knowing your value and how to be your authentic self is also

a self-care tactic that contributes to empowerment. Though

we certainly want to enhance all forms of diversity among

our staff, it requires a lot of deep and systemic work. Having

a candidate of color join your organization just to leave

within a few years or stay for a while but not show up every day as their unapologetic and authentic self is a malpractice, regardless of the salary that many affluent districts can provide. What good is a $10,000 - $30,000 raise if you must ultimately spend it on therapy just to cope with the trauma you may endure in a predominantly White school system?

As with each level, pushback is still there. Not everyone has arrived at the place on their journey where they can acknowledge educational inequities, yet not doing anything about educational inequities continues to be one of the biggest barriers in our field. Inequities that serve as barriers to our students' success are too often approached by well-meaning believers in equity work looking for a win-win compromise for everyone to move forward as a unit. Understand that we are currently living the compromise, and frankly the compromise is simply decorated inequities. This is the reason why I define educational equity as creating or eliminating. If you are not creating or eliminating, in other words engaged in action, you are complicit in inequities. We have enough equity philosophers and people who can tell you what needs to happen when they interview, or when you ask, but who also waited until they retired or left the field of education to become voiced on equity matters. Some are still fearful and unwilling to impact policies, practices, and systems.

The good news is that all these forms of pushback and complicity have become predictable. As a result, if you are serious about achieving educational equity within your schools; you can anticipate and strengthen your equity efforts which will enhance the likelihood of success. (If you are a district level official or part of a senior leadership team and you are fighting for equity and would like to form a support group as you continue or consider impacting systems within your organization, scan the QR code below to join the

"District Leaders for Educational Equity" GroupMe, which is dedicated to such work.)

State-Level

By May 2020, Black Males in Education - St. Louis (BMESTL) was recognized as a major player in St. Louis as an educational advocacy and empowerment organization. Though it had only been a year since Dr. Darryl Diggs Jr. and I co-founded BMESTL, we were able to lead initiatives that focused on recruiting, developing, supporting, retaining, and mentoring Black educators as an avenue to invest in students. Even with the success of two symposiums (The State of Black Educators Symposium), two published books (Voices by BMESTL Vol. 1 and 2), the creation of multiple avenues for Black educators to convene and be supported, and a memorandum of understanding that focuses on Inclusion, Diversity, Equity, Antibias, and Antiracism in educational and nonprofit organizations, we were still being complicit in educational inequities by underestimating our influence.

In July 2020, BMESTL held a state-wide meeting to discuss issues related to Black students and educators in the state of Missouri. With representation from St. Louis, Kansas City, Columbia, and Jefferson City, where the meeting was held, a "table" was created for Black males to strategize and mobilize a collective plan to increase representation and accountability when educational decisions are being made. This meeting was also attended by representatives from the DESE, including the Commissioner of Education. Through discussion, the group generated a few recommendations for enhancing the state's equity efforts which included allowing a few Black males to present at a State Board Meeting.

On October 20, 2021, Dr. Diggs and I presented at the Missouri State Board of Education Meeting. Our 10-minute presentation and 12-minute response to questions from board members focused on equity, policy, and the Missouri School Improvement Program (MSIP). Though we commended DESE for making strides towards equity, we challenged them to do more; including quantifying equity efforts to increase implementation and accountability. We also pleaded for them to become more intentional in recruiting Black educators into the field.

At the January 12, 2021 Missouri State Board of Education Meeting, an official from DESE mentioned Dr. Diggs and me by name, referenced our October presentation, then expounded on how one of our recommendations would inform their ongoing equity and access efforts for the state. None of this would have been possible without leveraging our influence to disrupt inequitable systems.

Though this was certainly an honor, our work is nowhere near done. As Dr. Diggs mentioned in the Foreword, our best ideas to advance this work have yet to be seen.

How do you apply the
INITIAL ACTION STEPS
at you current level?

Let us know on social media
by using the hashtag,
#AchieveEduEquity.

Step 1: Ask Yourself, "Am I Being Complicit in Educational Inequities?"

Step 2: Identify Educational Inequities

Step 3: Challenge Existing Equity Efforts & Barriers to Strengthen/Systematize

Step 4: Throw Away Superficial, Trash Equity

Step 5: Wash Your Hands

Step 6: Repeat Steps 1-5 and Bring a Friend

Dr.Howard Fields .com   ActionableEQUITY.com

Having Said That...

Achieving educational equity requires sacrifice. After writing the preceding chapters of this book while also reflecting on my experiences, I have come to the realization that all organizations can take the initial steps to achieve educational equity. Having said that, it hurts me to admit that I do not believe educational equity, as defined as creating and/or eliminating policies, systems, and practices in schools that impact the experiences, outcomes, and access to resources for students from previously excluded groups, will proceed beyond the initial steps in most organizations.

Educators may believe in educational equity as a concept, but as an application, I am not convinced. The coordination, leadership, accountability, humility, dedication, and ultimately sacrifice required to go beyond the initial action steps continues to expose the hypocrisy in our field. We are making things more difficult than they should be, but this is not an accident. Even during a time when a pandemic has shown us that we have the capability to drastically change the way we educate students, educational inequities have gotten worse. I believe this to be the case because we move the goal post, so to speak, with great regularity anytime we are tasked with addressing educational inequities. Additionally, we overplay the notion that "we are trying to address these problems, but it takes time."

When these beliefs are articulated and we do not pushback or challenge it, we are betraying our students who need us the most. Accepting this narrative, especially at the teacher level, principal level, district level, and state level, we commit ourselves to be complicit in educational inequities. Change in education only tends to take a substantial amount of time when there is a conflict of interest. Too often, that conflict has been the absence of accountability measures in educational equity along with politics. Allow me to illustrate some practices we must eliminate if we are serious about going beyond the initial steps of educational equity.

Teacher Level

Earlier in my educational career, I was under the assumption that all school systems progress monitored (check and monitors student progress), collaborated, and utilized research-based strategies to inform their instruction. I now wonder if these practices are reserved for school systems that serve large populations of students of color, students who receive special education services, and schools that serve a large number of students who qualify for free or reduced-priced meals.

We like to paint the picture that educators must decide to be either data-informed or student-centered. Simply a tactic to shy away from accountability, I would argue that you cannot be student-centered if you are not also using data to inform your instruction.

Too often, I see teachers who have been vocal in their support of educational equity, yet they do not know how their students are performing at any given time in their class or if they do know, there are minimal if any; instructional adjustments made. Loving your students while refusing to adjust your teaching to better align with their individual needs is nothing more than a form of gift-wrapped educational neglect.

I have also seen learning models that provide students with additional supports but at the expense of their tier one instruction (instruction provided by their primary teacher). If students receive added support, with a less qualified staff member, during the time their primary teacher is providing the same or similar instruction to other members of the class, unless this arrangement is part of an individualized education plan (IEP), it is no longer supplemental support. Unfortunately, we do things like this and later wonder why these same students are not performing as well as we would like.

We must also eliminate the practice of not discussing and sharing data as a form of protecting teachers. By no means does this mean we "beat teachers up over their data," but this does mean we need to discuss their students' growth or lack thereof, then provide the necessary guidance and support to the teacher. If teachers are receptive and display the willingness to become more effective for all of their students, we proceed accordingly. But if teachers cannot engage or reflect on their students' performance in a meaningful way, allowing them to continue to harm kids becomes an issue the principal and leaders in the district must address. If you believe publishing results by teachers is not nice, just imagine how those schools who have been identified as being among the lowest 5-10 percent feel. In fact, there are currently legislative bills in the Missouri Senate and House that expand on the accountability of these schools.

Principal Level

I have a statement regarding leadership that is quite polarizing but true; the only thing missing in leadership, are leaders. If a principal cannot move the students and staff they are tasked with leading, forward; they should not be there. Based on my experiences, many leaders do not like to be held accountable but want to hold others accountable. The interesting thing about accountability is that I was always at my best as a leader when I knew someone was watching and expecting great things from my leadership. When there is no accountability, things that should not matter as much begin to dictate what the leader focuses on.

Within the context of equity, all systems should hold themselves accountable to the same term they use with regularity to show they care (equity). But care without action is complicity. I need you to care enough to embed equity into your improvement plans. I need you to care enough to address the inequitable practices in your schools. I need you to care enough that you stop being afraid of parents who you hear from often that engage in opportunity hoarding. We must hold ourselves to a higher standard. As I think about the successes I had as a principal, what makes it more rewarding is it validates the time and sometimes pain that I went through as a building leader. Whether I was in a financially challenged or affluent space, I upset people. There were people who did not like me. Some even did all they could to influence others to feel the same. I have had supervisors who were threatened by the passion, intensity, and tenacity I brought to any room when discussing students and matters of equity. I disrupted systems, increased accountability for staff, and even respectfully challenged superiors when necessary. I did it all, realizing that is what it takes if you want to achieve educational equity. It was hard. It was lonely. Possessing the knowledge of what is necessary in order to move a building and school community forward, only to see so many leaders not willing to make the same sacrifice because they are comfortable or selfishly protecting something or someone is the disappointment that almost caused me to leave the profession.

Most equity efforts are performative at best because leaders want the equity that everyone will agree to. The kind where no one will resist. This type of equity is called, say it with me, - trash equity.

It is time to remove this mindset because it is ultimately harming kids. The question I will leave for those at the principal level is this; if not making sufficient progress towards educational equity could result in you being nonrenewed, would you be out of a job?

District Level

I once heard Dr. Mark Bedell, Superintendent of Kansas City Public Schools say, "people obtain leadership positions then stop doing the things that got them hired." This statement is aligned with my beliefs related to leadership. Though it can be challenging, leadership is also rewarding. For me, the most rewarding part is continuing to make student-centered decisions while also advancing educational equity, regardless of the cost.

I was once told that one of the scariest places in education is the intersection of education and politics. Unfortunately for educational equity, when used beyond a superficial manner, it is interwoven with the acknowledgment of systemic racism. The term "students from previously excluded groups" does support the claim that race has played a role in students being historically excluded from educational opportunities. When leaders are not willing to discuss race or implement possible solutions that reference race because of political reasons, they quickly lose credibility.

The consolation prize is either trash equity measures or a laundry list of excuses and reasons to delay implementing matters associated with educational equity. In the words of former Prime Minister of the United Kingdom, William E. Gladstone, "justice delayed is justice denied."

Ever since Brown v. Board of Education (1954), the education system continues to delay any progressive adoptions to enhance the chance that educational equity persists in our schools. All because of fear. If we continue to view any progressive step towards enhancing the possibility of success for our students who have been previously excluded through a political lens, we fall victim to a scarcity mentality in education. District leaders and boards of education have the responsibility to make student-centered decisions, regardless of how difficult the decision may be or who may not like it.

State Level

If we were as serious as we like for people to believe we are about achieving educational equity, there would be educational equity in the legislature. Specifically, there would be a law for all districts or local educational agencies (LEAs) to adopt educational equity policies. The Missouri School Board Association (MSBA) would recommend educational equity policies for districts to adopt and there would be more than only a few school districts with policies that show their commitment to educational equity. While I am optimistic that DESE will begin assessing schools and districts on their ability to achieve educational equity, I also know these same issues have been around for some time. Though the small incremental discussions related to educational equity have started, I am still unaware of similar discussions and plans to address the Eurocentric, single-story curriculum that permeates many school systems. What would be the impact if districts and LEAs were awarded points on their APR for diversifying their curriculum and staff? Better yet, instead of creating legislative bills that call for publishing the lowest 5-10 percent of schools, what if we published the top 5-10 percent of schools causing racial trauma to students based on the Office of Civil Rights data or student survey data? What if districts were penalized when their teachers engage in harmful and demeaning behavior toward students? It appears that every measure that is currently assessed rewards affluent schools for being affluent and penalizes poor schools for being poor. In the case of public schools in St. Louis, Kansas City, Springfield, and Columbia, these same measures tend to reward schools with low populations of Black and Brown students while penalizing public schools with high populations of Black and Brown students. But as I stated earlier, what has already been illustrated in this chapter serves as just some of the practices we must eliminate if we are serious about going beyond the initial steps of educational equity.

Achieving Educational Equity Audit

We all have various levels of optimism, and pessimism for that matter, when it comes to the equity efforts of our educational organizations. Regardless, I encourage you to find a way to do your part to help achieve educational equity. If you do not know where to start, this chapter will provide you with a pathway to engage. If you have done some equity work with your team but now you are stuck, this chapter is also for you.

Years ago, I searched everywhere for an educational equity audit but was unable to find anything that adequately addressed the needs of the building I was leading. Using the vast array of experiences I have obtained in this area since then, what follows is an audit to assess the educational equity efforts that exist within your organization.

After completing this audit, you should have a better understanding of where your organization currently stands in achieving educational equity. Additionally, the inquiry-based approach provides enough questions for any individual or group of individuals to use as a guide to advance educational equity within their organization.

(Please note that throughout this audit, I use the term "organization." Though this term could mean your entire institution, it could also mean your school, department, team, grade level, etc. As you continue to revisit and re-engage with this audit, the purpose is to eventually be able to assess the educational equity efforts of the entire organization, district, or LEA.)

Declarative Statements

Retrieve all the statements your organization uses to guide their work. Often called mission statements, vision statements, value statements, and shared commitments, to name a few, these statements assist the organization with decision making. Search for the term equity in these documents. If it is there, access the definition and compare it to the educational equity definition used in this book. What are the similarities and differences among the definitions? If there is not a definition, create or adopt one. How often are these declarative statements referenced? Do all stakeholders, including students, take ownership of these statements?

If your organization has clearly defined educational equity, references it in your declarative statements, and has evidence to support there is ownership of these statements, your organization is proficient in this area.

Improvement Plans

Review your strategic plan and/or comprehensive school improvement plan. Is equity explicitly referenced in these documents? If so, are there specific action plans that focus on creating or eliminating policies, practices, and systems? Are there specific strategies included to impact the experiences, outcomes, and access to resources? If not, create or adopt strategies that introduce these concepts. Do the plans provide an accountability measure to ensure the improvement plan timeline is being adhered to?

If your organization includes equity in your improvement plans as well as your action steps, your organization is proficient in this area.

Governance

Search for the word "equity" in your organizational policies, code of conduct, governance plans, and any other documents that provides information related to how the organization will govern. Focus on results that only reference equity within the context of educational equity (many board policies references equity as it relates to revenue and financial conflicts of interest).

Assess what is discoverable from these documents. Determine the alignment between what is written and what is occurring within the organization. If there is a policy or document that references educational equity, can it be observed in action? Are there any accountability measures embedded within these documents? Are there any organizational documents that allow employees to have a choice not to adhere to these documents as it pertains to equity? How often and when are these documents referenced? What are the success indicators? How is adequate progress deduced?

If your organization has adopted educational equity in its governance documents, has clearly defined what success or growth looks like in this area, and has accountability measures embedded to ensure implementation, your organization is proficient in this area.

Communication

The previous three sections are the foundational blocks to being serious about achieving educational equity within the organization. At a bare minimum, you must be proficient in those areas if your goal is to go beyond the initial steps of educational equity. Unfortunately, when it comes to equity, performative acts that give the impression of significant progress towards equity is a common occurrence. It is because of this, many of the following sections will provide insight and assess exactly how serious an organization is in achieving educational equity. We will start with communication.

How often are the previous three sections communicated to all stakeholders? Where are these documents communicated? Is it easily accessible on the website, in the schools, in meetings, on the communication that is sent home to students?

In addition to the leaders, are teachers, support staff, students, and the community aware of the organization's commitment to educational equity? Taking it a step further, when the organization communicates in general, is there a concerted effort to consider the perspective and experiences of previously excluded groups? Do the communication channels (access to information) reinforce inequities that exist within the organization?

If your organization has an easily accessible plan that communicates the previous three sections to all stakeholders in a matter that considers the perspective and experiences of those who have been previously excluded, your organization is proficient in this area.

Learning

Conduct an age-appropriate survey that asks students if they believe they have the necessary resources to be successful in class. Ask if there are any current rules or procedures that impact their learning. Determine what learning experiences get them excited about coming to school (or logging in) as well as what learning experiences do not make them want to come to school (or login) every day. Try to assess if the lessons they experience liberate or oppress them. Do they provide positive reinforcement and acceptance of who they are, or do they conform to certain negative stereotypes? Be sure to explicitly ask if they observe any inequities within the school. (You may say that many students may not have a firm understanding of what inequities are. I would respond, neither do most educators.) If student do identify inequities, continue probing. Ask more questions to gather more insight in order to understand their perspective.

Conduct a similar survey for parents and staff. Make sure you establish a way to review the survey results by various groups (i.e., students, parents, staff, grade, race, etc.). What does the data suggest? Are there any perceived inequities from participants? How will you communicate and use the data?

The goal is not to have what would be described as perfect or positive survey results. The goal is to elicit organic feedback and be reflective.

If your organization conducts a survey that elicits the previously mentioned information, reflects on the data, and creates a responsive, time-bound plan of action to addresses undesirable narratives and themes from the data, your organization is proficient in this area.

Grading/Feedback

There are several books that do a fantastic job of examining equitable grading practices. Select one and engage in a book study. (Remember, if your book study does not lead to creating or eliminating policies, systems, or practices, it is trash.)

For the purposes of the audit, let us focus our attention on the manner in which your organization receives feedback on its current equity efforts.

Are all stakeholders allowed to provide feedback? Is there an equity committee? Are they consulted on any matter related to equity? What happens when they pushback on ideas? Are students and parents allowed to provide feedback to teachers regarding how equity shows up in their work? Are they allowed to provide feedback on the school's equity efforts? If your organization is proficient in the communication section of the audit, stakeholders may already be familiar with the efforts and their perspective would be an excellent data source to examine the effectiveness of such plans. Do supervisors provide feedback to their staff on their equity efforts? Is equity a measure being documented on evaluations as a practical matter?

If your organization has a system for consistently providing feedback to staff on their equity efforts as well as receiving feedback from staff, students, parents, and community, on the organization's equity efforts, your organization is proficient in this area.

Data/Outcomes

This section is of critical significance for any organization that is serious about achieving educational equity. For starters, does your organization have a protocol that is used throughout the system for collecting, reviewing, and reflecting on data produced by the district and their staff? Is the data disaggregated into subgroups? Are leaders, teachers, and applicable support staff expected to use data to inform their decisions? What are the accountability measures? Is there a multi-tiered system of supports for students who are needing to improve? Is there a multi-tiered system of supports for teachers, administrators, and entire schools that are needing to improve their outcomes or understanding of using data to inform their instruction and/or decisions? Does your organization not only review data from standardized tests but also data related to advanced courses, gifted education, teacher referrals, graduations, surveys, etc.? Are actionable and timely plans created to address trends within the data? Is there a culture of taking ownership of data?

If your organization utilizes a system for collecting, reviewing, reflecting, and acting on data received to improve, disaggregates such data into subgroups, provides support for students, staff, and schools who need support, and fosters a culture of data ownership, your organization is proficient in this area.

Leadership

Do the members of your organization, especially the leaders, have a robust understanding of educational equity? Do they have experience leading and making decisions in an equitable manner? Are they open to growing in this area? Do they feel a sense of urgency when making decisions that impact educational equity? Have they ever created or eliminated policies, systems, or practices that impact the experiences, outcomes, and access to resources for students from previously excluded groups? Do they know how to create or eliminate policies, systems, and practices? Are they strong enough to create or eliminate policies, systems, and practices? Are their words regarding educational equity aligned with their actions related to educational equity and vice versa? Do they view educational equity as a top priority?

If a significant amount of the organization's leadership team has a robust understanding of educational equity, a sense of urgency, experience creating or eliminating policies, systems, or practices that impact the experiences, outcomes, and access to resources for students from previously excluded groups, and if they consistently align their words and actions related to equity, your organization is proficient in this area.

Professional Learning

Is educational equity representative in the professional learning plans? Does your organization partner with leaders in equity work to enhance the learning for staff? Is there alignment with the learning and application of educational equity? Is there accountability with the learning and application of educational equity? Is the learning related to educational equity mandatory or optional? Is credit provided to those who take it upon themselves to advance their learning in educational equity? Is credit provided to those who lead educational equity efforts for other members of the organization. Is there an educational improvement plan for those who are struggling with implementing educational equity practices?

If your organization mandates educational equity in their professional learning plans while also measuring it to provide credit or additional support for staff depending upon how they respond, your organization is proficient in this area.

(Do not forget to check out the educational equity professional learning plan included in the additional resources section. The plan can assist in this area and includes a micro credential credit option.)

Interviewing

Has your organization spent time developing a procedure to hire candidates who are strong in educational equity or candidates who have the potential to be strong in educational equity? Has the interview process been scrutinized through the lens of educational equity? Are there opportunities to dissect interview responses to shy away from candidates who only speak of educational equity in a deficit model as opposed to an asset model? Have the individuals who are serving on the interview panel invested in enough equity work on their own to accurately assess the equity responses of potential candidates? Are assessments conducted with staff members regarding implementation of the organization's educational equity efforts?

If your organization has developed an intentional interview process to hire candidates who are strong or have the potential to be strong in educational equity and the interview panel can accurately assess the equity responses of potential candidates, your organization is proficient in this area.

Decision Making

Is educational equity at the forefront of all decisions you make as an organization? Are there guiding questions that pertain to educational equity anytime decisions are being made? Who is spearheading the most recent educational equity work? Is there any apprehension? How is the apprehension being handled? Are matters associated with educational equity handled differently than other matters? Is educational equity annexed or is it part of all decisions?

Though this section does not include a scoring component, it should be a constant point of emphasis within the organization.

Expenditures

Are educational equity efforts adequately funded? Review the expenditures of the organization's initiatives. Where does educational equity efforts rank? Are the consultants and resources used to further educational equity efforts within the organization paid at a commensurate level to other efforts the organization is committed to? What is the current budget for educational equity? Are staff members who lead and implement educational equity efforts adequately funded or compensated? Are other purchased services made with educational equity in mind? Review the top/most frequently used vendors for the organization. What is their stance on equity? How do they work to ensure equity within their organization? Do they employ individuals from previously excluded groups? Historically, what percentage of the organizations' expenditures in purchased services go to minoritized business enterprises? How often does the organization promote or reach out to minoritized business enterprises for the purposes of purchase services? Does the organization's expenditures support or conflict with their belief in educational equity?

If your organization adequately funds educational equity efforts, tracks spending, and attempts to align it with educational equity beliefs, engages in conversation with vendors they most frequently do business with to obtain their beliefs related to educational equity, your organization is proficient in this area.

(EduOpenings.com has the capability for organizations to connect with minoritized business enterprises.)

Continuous Improvement

How often are matters related to equity revisited? When was the last equity audit? Do members of your organization engage in educational equity learning walks? Are you collaborating with other organizations to continue improvement in educational equity? Do you have any explicit educational equity goals? Has there been any evidence to support progress towards those goals? How do you determine adequate improvement in your educational equity efforts? Is there a substantial improvement in all quantifiable learning outcomes for students? What does the data suggest as it relates to staff implementation of educational equity efforts? Does the organization strongly encourage staff to obtain micro credentials in educational equity? How do staff, students, parents, and the community rate your educational equity efforts? How will you use this data? What did the achieving educational equity audit reveal about your organization? How will you respond to this?

If your organization tracks its progress related to educational equity, immediately responds to the data, continues to set educational equity goals, and assesses the progress of those goals, your organization is proficient in this area.

ACHIEVING EDUCATIONAL EQUITY AUDIT

	Trash	Proficient
Declarative Statements:		
Improvement Plans:		
Governance:		
Communication:		
Learning:		
Grading/Feedback:		
Data/Outcomes:		
Leadership:		
Professional Learning:		
Interviewing:		
Decision Making:		
Expenditures:		
Continuous Improvement:		

After completing the audit, determine which area(s)
are trash for your organization and W.A.S.H. your hands.

Post-Pandemic Schooling

In the coming months, I anticipate we will begin to see more published comprehensive reports on the impact the global pandemic had on schools. One area of particular interest for me will be the lens through which these reports are presented. Will the same narrative prevail related to how "those" schools are failing without mentioning how under-resourced they are or how nearly every measurement tool used to assess them is inherently inequitable?

On more than one occasion, I remember being frustrated by the way in which schools and districts were being held accountable. During my time as a principal, my colleagues and I often pleaded our case as to why policies, systems, and practices needed to change. We felt the current conditions penalized us for school location and for lacking the resources to consistently address the competing priorities associated with urban education.

In 2020, the COVID-19 pandemic forced the entire field of education to change policies, systems, and practices that had been previously used for centuries to educate students.

One of those changes included flexibility in the way attendance is reported. Schools were no longer required to make up lost or canceled days of school up to 36 hours. It could be considered "exceptional or emergency circumstances" if they had an approved Alternative Methods of Instruction plan. This was a shift from seven years ago when a school I was leading experienced an exceptional and emergency circumstance.

During the 2014-2015 school year, our district consistently communicated the attendance goal; 90 percent of students in attendance 90 percent of the time. Our school was well below this mark with only 79 percent of students in attendance 90 percent of the time at one point. Such a low attendance percentage was due to the Ferguson Unrest. When you are attempting to regain district accreditation, attendance points are a must-have. I do not recall if our attendance was held against us that year or not through the hold harmless provision, but my point is that it took a global pandemic to make such a massive systemic shift in education. Let us continue the trend of massive educational shifts and make some additional structural changes to help our students and school communities.

School Suspensions

Though the utilization and implementation of virtual learning may have started off terrible for some, we have nearly mastered the art of providing learning opportunities for students who are engaged remotely. Because of this, I believe we should ban out of school suspensions for non-Safe School violations. Understand I do believe in providing a separate setting only when absolutely necessary, but with the emergence of Zoom, Google Meet, Webex and Skype, what would it look like for students who prefer online learning or for students who are removed from in-person learning temporarily to remain engaged virtually? Even if online learning attendance credit was not commensurate to that of in-person attendance credit, I believe that should become the new norm. The days of sending students home and not providing them with at minimum a virtual learning option should be abolished.

Anti-Racism and Anti-Hate Practices

Being a Black male with a diverse social network, a diverse group of friends, and a diverse family, I sometimes feel the only place that is not open to discussing diversity beyond a safe level is our schools. We all know what gets measured gets done. Though I do see us eventually moving past the COVID-19 pandemic, I am not as hopeful that we will be able to move past the racism and hate pandemic due to our coddling, back door dealings, and low- key acceptance of these practices. It is time for federal and state education departments to require schools to properly educate our students, staff, and school communities about racism and hate. Many students and staff members are experiencing each of these matters before, during, and after school but cannot openly discuss their concerns. The work in these efforts is even more paramount in school systems that are not racially or ethnically diverse; to ensure that students are accepting of cultures and people they may be less likely to encounter in their schools.

Curriculum, Instruction, and Assessment Overhaul

As an extension of the previous section, there is a common belief that diversifying their staff is the best way to expose students to diversity within their schools. While this is "a" way, it is not the "only" way. Otherwise, it becomes a problem as well as missed opportunities when schools ignore the power in diversifying the people and cultures in the lessons and materials in which they expose to students. Some school communities are not diverse at all, yet they may also be dedicated to eliminating single-story narratives. All school systems, leaders, and principals have varying degrees of autonomy and can contribute to a curriculum and instructional overhaul as it relates to diversity. It should be against the law for any student to never see themselves and their family as protagonists (or to only see themselves and their family as protagonists) in the materials used to educate them and prepare them for the world.

Furthermore, we must push for all assessments to be more representative of all students, all learning styles and all cultures. Because the standardized tests have not been as consistent as of late, why not entertain the notion of allowing schools and educators to showcase their students' mastery by publishing work in the most organic, creative, and relevant ways?

Being a curriculum, instruction, and assessment enthusiast, if we spend more time directing our efforts and energy in this manner instead of continuing to examine our students who have been previously excluded through a deficit model; the pandemic could consequently end up being the change we so desperately yearned for in education.

Student-Centered and Equity-Focused

I remember making calls to my families in the summer of 2013. The recent Breitenfeld v. Clayton court ruling meant that many of my students I was planning to loop with and become their assistant principal for a second consecutive year now had the option to transfer to a fully accredited school district. For some families, I was able to convince them to stay. For others, my persuasive pitch was not enough. Though I had amazing relationships with my students and parents, the reality was that our school district was unaccredited. Even though they may have admired their child's former physical education teacher who was now their assistant principal, the opportunity to attend a high performing district with more resources was too much to pass up for some.

I would later learn that the reason many students stayed at our school was because their families knew they could depend on our staff to always put students first. Twelve months later I would become a building principal.

Due to student performance the years prior to my arrival at Koch, I frequently met with representatives from DESE to discuss school improvement plans. What I remember most about those meetings was learning how much leadership mattered. When leaders have high expectations of students, are unapologetic in their commitment, and if they can cultivate these same characteristics in their staff, they will enhance learner outcomes for students. The blueprint was established. Based on every quantifiable measure -- including our school's climate and culture survey results, it was confirmed that student-centered, yet equity-focused leadership could "move mountains."

I remember defending scheduling changes in 2017 that provided students with more elective course options and teachers with common plan time to collaborate, just as vividly as I remember reaching out to families in 2018 to make them aware of space we had at our lottery-based elementary school that would allow their child (ren) to walk to their neighborhood school instead of being bussed across the district.

All of these examples illustrate decisions that were students-centered and equity-focused. Each one took my mental and emotional capacity to the edge, but as I look back, I realize regardless of the school, regardless of the year, and regardless of the situation, students, staff, and school communities need leaders who are student-centered and equity-focused. When you respond to the individual needs of each individual student, they will exceed all expectations. I absolutely love my students. But most of them did not need my love. What they needed was my grace, belief in them, and influence to remove barriers that stood in the way of them being afforded a fulfilling and prosperous life. This cannot happen if you dismiss the premise of educational equity.

In a few months, I will speak on behalf of Missouri students and principals at the 2021 National Association of Elementary School Principals Conference. In my limited time at the podium, I plan to inspire leaders from across the country to create and eliminate policies, systems, and practices in schools that impact the experiences, outcomes, and access to resources for students, families, colleagues, and communities I/they/we took an oath to serve. Many of which have been previously excluded from opportunities to succeed. They trusted my leadership enough to allow me to grow, learn, and evolve into the leader I am today. The irony is that by serving school communities and going above and beyond to make sure they never have to endure some of the challenges I faced as a student, I am able to provide for my family and invest in other leaders. This is my motivation.

And the only fear I have, besides God, is facing a student, parent, colleague, or community member who depended on my leadership only to let them know that I could not make a difficult decision or impact necessary change because it would have threatened my selfish interests. If this were to occur, I would have essentially been modeling what I despise; weak leadership.

Understand that I have never had all the answers. I have never been without flaws. One of my most valuable assets, however, is my ability to reflect, learn, and grow. That stated, I feel it is my responsibility to do all I can for students.

In education, this often equates to speaking truth to power. As you can imagine, this also sometimes equates to being labeled, unaccepted, uninvited, not promoted, in (good) trouble, and many other things that come with remaining student-centered and equity-focused. But there is a perk to being this way; the abundance of peace that comes with unapologetic authenticity. I do not feel the need to be anyone but the best version of me when I enter a space. This does not mean I will not continue to evolve. It simply means I have arrived at a place where intrinsic harmony and intrinsic approval is what I seek. If you have had such a feeling, you know there is not a job or salary alone that can provide this. In fact, I would rather lose a job and find myself than lose myself for a job. Therefore, the passion and sense of urgency you may feel while reading these words, is the same passion and sense of urgency I hope you will use to help achieve educational equity for the students, staff, and school communities you have been blessed to serve.

ADDITIONALRESOURCES

AUTHOR'S TALK
Dr. Fields expands on the book and next steps
for how to achieve educational equity.

PROFESSIONAL LEARNING PLAN
A practical framework created for those interested in
continuing to work towards educational equity.

MICRO CREDENTIAL CREDIT
Complete the Professional Learning Plan, along with
a 15 minute presentation and 500 word essay for credit.

MINI PODCAST
Learn from others as they share where they
are on their respective educational equity journey.

EDUCATIONAL EQUITY BLOG POSTS
Access multiple blog posts by Dr. Fields on
the topic of educational equity.

DISCOUNTED CONSULTING
10% off of Dr. Fields' consulting services.

Access these resources at:
drhowardfields.com/EDUequity

About the Author

 Dr. Howard E. Fields III currently serves as an Assistant Superintendent of Human Resources and is the co-founder of Black Males in Education St. Louis (BMESTL) and EduOpenings.com. He is also the 2020 National Elementary Distinguished Principal from Missouri. Dr. Fields' leadership was responsible for navigating the Ferguson Unrest, increasing his school's Annual Performance Report (APR) by 200 percent in his first year as a principal. This was among the highest growth of any North St. Louis County public elementary school in 2015. In 2017, Dr. Fields was internationally recognized by the Networked Digital Library of Theses and Dissertations for the innovativeness of his research. Accompanying his 132-page dissertation was a feature-length documentary on the topic of Missouri's Student Transfer Law, a law that forced unaccredited school districts to pay the tuition and transportation costs for students who decided to transfer from their home district to attend an accredited school district in the same or adjoining district. In 2020, Dr. Fields co-founded the inaugural State of Black Educators Symposium, an event created to increase the recruitment, support, mentorship, and development of Black educators. Dr. Fields has authored several articles and has been highlighted in national publications such as *Education Week* and *Principal Leadership*, and consistently shares his knowledge and expertise while presenting both nationally and regionally. You can connect with Dr. Fields on Twitter at @HeFields3 or by placing your cell phone camera on the QR code below to access his Linktree.

Notes:

Bonus Equity

According to a 2016 report by the Center for Public Education, (educational) equity is achieved when all students receive the resources they need so they graduate prepared for success after high school. In this same report, the National School Board Association stated, public schools should provide equitable access and ensure that all students have the knowledge and skills to succeed as contributing members of a rapidly changing, global society, regardless of factors such as race, gender, sexual orientation, ethnic background, English proficiency, immigration status, socioeconomic status, or disability. A question that was included in this same report for leaders who are interested in making their schools equitable was, are your students college and career-ready?"

"College and career-ready" have consistently been used to mean raising academic standards by emphasizing excellence. However, with the growing number of colleges and universities phasing out SAT and ACT scores as an admissions requirement, I wonder how we will quantify skills needed for students to be successful moving forward.

Currently, the overwhelming majority of rhetoric associated with academic excellence equates to high standardized test scores. But what if we cultivated an environment where we assessed our students' 21st-century skills (critical thinking, creativity, collaboration, communication, relevant content knowledge, courageousness, and consciousness of others)? What if we then took the results and created an individualized plan to complement their strengths and better prepare them to be college and career-ready? Once adequate progress is made, we could showcase their growth using various mediums. Such an event would help us provide a more well-rounded account of our students' learning, resilience, and skills. By inviting business leaders, college and career recruiters, education department personnel, families, and other applicable parties, students would be able to experience a microcosm of the world with countless possibilities to explore. This is the readiness we should want for all of our kids.

On the back cover of this book, there is a "painting" of my four kids. Each one of them has a gift. My oldest son is gifted academically, my daughter is gifted artistically, my middle son is gifted athletically, and my youngest son is already a gifted comedian. Though each will have different challenges and barriers they will undoubtedly face while matriculating through school and life, I pray the educators they will encounter along their journey will see them as I do.

I added an image of them because it serves as a reminder that every student I advocate for and hope to empower has a parent or guardian that loves and wants nothing less than the best for them. I want the same for my kids. Never would I give up on them or believe they do not have a chance at success. The same sentiment is shared regarding my students. Each one of them. Even in their non-ideal moments, I provide grace knowing that we are all better than our worst mistake.

Please extend this grace to yourselves as well. Regardless of where you are on your educational equity journey, know that our kids need you. In many regards, we are their hope. But if we do not do something about the current policies, systems, and practices that continue to have a negative impact on our students, we are passively co-signing on the systemic barriers that exist within our field. The answer to the question, are your students college and career-ready, is a lot easier to answer when you are actively working to achieve educational equity.